AF409619

Miss Sarah Brown

Daughter of
Abolitionist John Brown

A Biography by

Mary Miller Chiao

TABLE OF CONTENTS

INTRODUCTION

Deep in the heart of the Adirondack Mountains in North Elba, New York, lies the grave of abolitionist John Brown, hanged for his raid on Harpers Ferry, Virginia, in 1859. Beside him are his two sons, Oliver and Watson, who were killed in the attack.

Across the continent in Saratoga, California, is the grave of John Brown's second wife, and mother of thirteen of his children, Mary Ann Day Brown. She rests with her daughters, Sarah and Ellen, and Ellen's family, in the Madronia Cemetery beneath the "John Brown Mountain."

This is the story of one of John Brown's children, Sarah, who crossed the country by wagon train with her mother and other members of her family after their father's death, to start a new life in California. They eventually settled in the little town of Saratoga in the foothills of the Santa Cruz Mountains.

CHAPTER I

December 1880
Saratoga, California

In December 1880, Sarah Brown stood on top of Table Mountain above the town of Saratoga, California. She was thirty-four years old, a tall, straight-backed woman with clear blue eyes, her brown hair held loosely in a braid caught up at the nape of her neck. R. L. Higgins, a well-respected Santa Clara Valley realtor, stood beside her, showing his advertised 160-acre mountain ranch.

Sarah had arrived three days earlier from Rohnerville in Humboldt County, California, in the midst of a torrential rainstorm, and Mr. Higgins "advised her to wait a few days before attempting to see the place and invited her to his own home … The weather continued exceedingly disagreeable the heavy rains kept the mountain roads impassable …"[1]

When the weather cleared, Sarah and Higgins proceeded in horse and buggy up Lumber Street,[2] cutting over to Oak, and then ascending the muddy unimproved road round hairpin curves and dangerous drops. Finally, they reached their

---

[1] Diary of Lucy Higgins, Higgins Family Collection.
[2] Now Big Basin Way.

destination approximately three miles above the town of Saratoga at an elevation of nineteen hundred feet. "One comes on it suddenly through a winding way, made dark even at midday by madrones and redwoods. A lonelier spot man never saw; it seems cut off from the world..."[3] A cabin stood on the clearing and a small fruit orchard close by. "Not fifty feet from the doorstep the mountain plunges down in sheer descent for hundreds of feet, and there filling the ... horizon ... lies the whole of Santa Clara Valley"[4] and San Francisco Bay, Mount Tamalpais, Mount Diablo, Grizzly Peak, and more. Sarah was an artist, and the scenery and smells and sounds must have dazzled her senses.[5] What painting she could do on this mountain! Sarah also knew that the long trek up the mountain ensured that few visitors would find them, and they could be distanced from the notoriety that followed them.

The price of the property was $1,850. Sarah and her family had scraped together only $350; yet, Higgins accepted that small amount as the down payment on the Bohlman Road

---

[3] John Muir, Ed., *Picturesque California: The Rocky Mountains and the Pacific Slope* (New York: J. Dewin Co., 1888), 301-302.
[4] Ibid, 301–302.
[5] R. V. Garrod, *Saratoga Story* (Privately published, 1961), 21-22, "... One forgets he wants to eat with all that beauty before him."

Property.[6] Living on the mountain top, besides Sarah, would be her mother, Mary Ann Day Brown, her younger sister, Ellen, and Ellen's husband, James Fablinger, and their three small daughters.

---

[6] "John Brown's Widow, Visit to her Mountain Home Near San Jose," *San Francisco Chronicle*, April 10, 1881.

Miss Brown, daughter of John and Mary Brown, at the age of 35 years, approximately, at the date of the *San Francisco Chronicle* interview, "John Brown's Widow, Visit to Her Mountain Home near San Jose," April 10, 1881. Collection of the Saratoga Historical Foundation, Saratoga, California.

R. L. Higgins, Realtor. Higgins Family Collection.

Sketch of the Brown Cabin on Bohlman Road. Assumed to be from "John Brown's Widow, Visit to Her Mountain Home Near San Jose," *San Francisco Chronicle*, April 10, 1881. Collection of the Saratoga Historical Foundation, Saratoga, California.

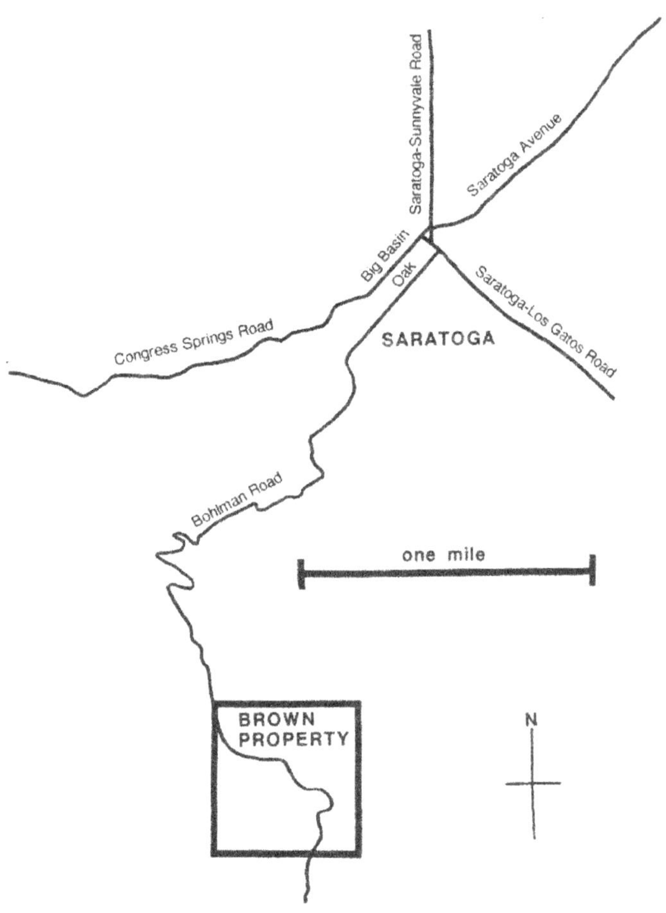

Map Credit: Nalty, Damon G., *The Browns of Madronia*. Saratoga, California: Saratoga Historical Foundation 1996.

CHAPTER II

1846 -1881
From Ohio to California

Sarah Brown was born in Akron, Ohio, on September 11, 1846, the seventeenth of twenty children sired by John Brown and the seventh by his second wife, Mary Ann Day. Sarah's father believed that slavery was against the laws of God and considered it his personal mission to eliminate it. When Sarah was nine, he moved his family to remote North Elba in the Adirondack Mountains of New York to live beside and assist black families farming at "Timbucto," a settlement financed by abolitionist Gerrit Smith[7] so that "every man that deserves a farm might have one."[8]

Sarah's father traveled frequently to obtain financing from abolitionists and to lead raids into Kansas and Missouri, during which he murdered pro-slavery men and freed slaves.[9] His family knew about his plans to seize the Federal Arsenal at

---

[7] Edward J. Renehan, Jr., *The Secret Six* (New York: Crown Publishers, Inc., 1995), 86.
[8] Edwin N. Cotter, Jr. quoting Gerrit Smith, "John Brown in the Adirondacks," *Adirondack Life Magazine,* Summer 1972.
[9] Renehan, 179.

Harpers Ferry, Virginia.[10] He believed that the townspeople would support him, and slaves would rise up everywhere seeking sanctuary at Harpers Ferry where they would be armed to continue the battle against slavery. Sarah, her mother, and the remaining family members waited in North Elba for his return. The raid failed. Ten men were killed, among them Sarah's two older brothers, Oliver and Watson. John Brown was hanged in December 1859.

"Considerable hardship was entailed when father left to engage in the Kansas warfare; but real poverty never obtruded itself until his death."[11] Mary Brown remained in North Elba with Sarah, 13, Annie, 16, and Ellen, 5. Her oldest son, Salmon, 23, lived nearby with his wife and family.

In 1860, educator Franklin Sanborn, one of John Brown's financial backers, visited Mrs. Brown and offered at no cost to educate Sarah and her older sister, Annie, at his school in Concord, Massachusetts. At that time, Concord, along with Boston, was the seat of the Transcendental Movement in America.

---

[10] In 1859, Harpers Ferry was located in Virginia. It became part of West Virginia in 1863 when West Virginia became the 35th state.

[11] Jean Libby, quoting Salmon Brown, "John Brown's Family and Their California Refuge," *The Californians* vol. 7, no. 1 (1989), 14.

> In the spring of 1860, my sister, Annie and myself were sent to Concord, Mass., to attend school. We first went to the home of Mr. Ralph Waldo Emerson … During the last year that I was in Concord, I boarded at Mr. Alcott's … Louisa, like her father, spent a good deal of her time in her room writing … Joining the Alcott's was … the home of Nathaniel Hawthorne … Miss Elizabeth Peabody was with them … I was in the habit of wandering around over the hills and often met Mr. Hawthorne … His eldest daughter … and I often took long walks to the many historical points of old Concord or out to Walden Pond … I seldom went to the post office without meeting Mr. Thoreau … I was often at his home …[12]

The children of prominent families such as the Emersons and Judge Rockwood Hoar[13] were Sarah's classmates. After two years, Mrs. Brown moved her to the Fort Edward Institute near Saratoga, New York, closer to home. Sarah seemed to have a natural talent for art, and she continued drawing and painting under Mary Artemesia Lathbury[14] … a pioneer in book and magazine illustration … a respected hymnist … one of the founders of the Chautauqua Movement.[15] Artist colonies abounded at that time in the Adirondacks, and the area was close to the Hudson River School Painters.

---

[12] Sarah Brown, "A Reminiscence," Collection of the Saratoga Historical Foundation.

[13] Tom Foran Clark, *The Significance of Being Frank*, http://www.ameribilia.com/sanborn/chapter8.html/ (February 22, 2005).

[14] "The Late Miss Sarah Brown," *San Jose Mercury Herald* (July 2, 1916), 24.

[15] Linda A. Moody, Mills College, "Religio-Political Insights of 19th Century Women Hymnists and Lyric Poets," Janus Head, http://www.janushead.org/JHSumm99/moody.cfm/ (March 12, 2005).

As the nation moved close to divided conflict, John Brown became a martyr of heroic proportions to the antislavery movement and a hated figure to those with pro-slavery sympathies. His family and his gravesite at the farm in North Elba became the focus of pilgrimages.

> Reformer Bronson Alcott hosted Mary Brown … People gathered outside, without invitations, straining to see members of John Brown's family … In Ohio, John Brown, Jr. complained of the great expense of handling the crowds that came to visit him. "Our house has been like a well-patronized hotel," he said. "Very many coming to see us from motives of pure curiosity." Others directed their curiosity and adulation toward the farm in North Elba, John Brown's burial site … July 4 became a day of pilgrimage for antislavery advocates. In 1860 more than 2000 people gathered at his grave.[16]

When Salmon and his wife planned to move to California, Mary made the decision that it would be difficult to remain in North Elba alone with the girls. She decided to accompany Salmon. " … Mary Brown also wanted to remove her daughters from the public attention that dogged them throughout New York and New England … She thought that going with Salmon 'would give Annie and Sarah a chance to do something for themselves in a new country that they cannot have here."[17] In 1863 the Browns joined a wagon train on the

---

[16] "John Brown's Family: A Living Legacy," *Civil War Times Magazine*, http://www.thehistorynet.com/ (February 25, 2005).
[17] Ibid.

Mormon Trail, connecting later to the Oregon and California Trails.

> It was a dangerous journey. Prior to the Civil War most of the regular troops were stationed on the frontier … these garrisons were transferred to the major theaters of war and their garrisons were taken over by less trained and less disciplined state militia units. The Indians soon realized the change … and became more bold … The Browns had one close call when Sioux warriors infiltrated their wagon train … there was another danger. It became known to the other families in the train that the family of John Brown was among them. Some were of Southern sympathy and John Brown was considered to be their hated foe. A plot was hatched to murder Salmon and perhaps even the women and children … They slipped away from that wagon train and eventually connected with another. Upon reaching the military post … Idaho, they informed the authorities … A detachment accompanied the Browns for nearly 200 miles until they were safely separated from those who would do them harm.[18]

In September 1864, Mary Ann, Sarah, Annie, Ellen, and Salmon Brown and his family arrived in Red Bluff, California. Sarah was 18 years old. They were penniless.

> The first winter in Red Bluff was an ordeal. Neighbors gave them food and clothing, and "calico parties" were held in Red Bluff and other communities, including Sacramento, to aid the Brown Family. Throughout her stay in Red Bluff, Mrs. Brown supported her family by serving as a nurse and midwife for the community.[19]

---

[18] Damon G. Nalty, *The Browns of Madronia* (Saratoga, California: Saratoga Historical Foundation, 1996), 9-10.

[19] "Unmarked Frame House in Red Bluff was Home of John Brown's Widow," *Sacramento Bee* (October 31, 1975).

The townspeople took up a collection and purchased land and built them a home.[20] Mary worked as a nurse,[21] and both Sarah and Annie taught school.

> Soon after they arrived in Red Bluff, Annie wrote in a letter: "Mother and Ellen will probably live in town, Sarah and I are going to teach school in the country." Records are a bit hazy as to which schools they might have taught in, but it seems pretty well established that one of them --- possibly both at different times --- taught at the Oat Creek School northwest of Tehama, a school mostly attended by black youngsters.[22] [23]

Sarah continued to paint. One of her paintings hangs today in the Kelly-Griggs House Museum in Red Bluff.[24] She may also have studied under California artist Charles Christian Nahl at this time.[25]

Sarah sought to augment her income by placing an ad in

---

[20] Lou Walther, "The Brown House," *Tehama County Memories 1990* (Red Bluff, California: Tehama County Genealogical and Historical Society, 1990), 19.

[21] Ibid., 17.

[22] Ibid., 18.

[23] "Oat Creek School," *Tehama County Memories 1987* (Red Bluff, California: Tehama County Genealogical and Historical Society, 1987), 72. "The Oat Creek School District was in the extreme western section of the Tehama County School District … It was founded in 1866 by P. D. Logan, a former slave who bought his freedom and became a rancher."

[24] "Unmarked Frame House in Red Bluff Was Home of John Brown's Widow," *Sacramento Bee* (October 31, 1975).

[25] *After Harper's Ferry* (Saratoga, California: Saratoga Historical Foundation, 1964), 14. "Years later, in the early 1880's, the art work was to be continued under the famous California artist, Charles Nahl," attributed to Mary Fablinger, niece of Sarah Brown. Although Nahl could very well have taught Sarah Brown in the Sacramento area, it would have been during the period 1864 to 1878, not in the 1880's. Nahl died in 1878.

the paper: "Miss S. Brown informs the ladies of Red Bluff and vicinity that she is prepared to do all kinds of stamping and marking for the purposes of embroidery. Having recently obtained many new and original designs, she hopes to give entire satisfaction to all who desire her services."[26]

The Brown family became close friends with artist Helen Tanner Brodt. "She was camped in the Sierra when the Browns came through. From daguerreotypes and under Mrs. Brown's guidance, Mrs. Brodt painted John Brown's portrait in oil. His widow pronounced it the best likeness ever done of him."[27]

The Browns were local celebrities since their arrival, but their presence politically divided the town. "From the first, there had been opposition to her and her family from slave state sympathizers, led by Red Bluff Sentinel editor Abe Townsend --- As the years went by, editor Townsend's attacks grew increasingly irritating."[28]

In 1870, Salmon's sheep-raising venture proved so successful he decided to move across the mountains to Rohnerville in Humboldt County where he could purchase more land and increase his herd. Mary decided to accompany

---

26 *Red Bluff Independent* (April 24, May 1, May 8, 1876).
27 Walther, "The Brown House," 81.
28 Ibid., 19.

him, and the family moved to Rohnerville, along with Annie's new husband, Samuel Adams.[29]

In Rohnerville, Mary continued as a midwife, and Sarah taught school. She continued painting and moved in with Salmon to home school his children in art and music. Ellen married schoolteacher, James Fablinger. Although Salmon was doing financially well, Sarah, her mother, and Ellen and James were not. In addition, Rohnerville was cold, windy, and foggy, and James Fablinger was not robust. In the winter of 1880, Mrs. Brown sent Sarah to look at the mountain property in Saratoga, and "owing to several causes, her son-in-law's ill health among others, she decided to remove to a milder climate, and fixed upon Santa Clara Valley."[30] In December 1880, Sarah departed from Rohnerville to Saratoga.

---

[29] Ibid., 20.

[30] "John Brown's Widow, Visit to Her Mountain Home Near San Jose," *The San Francisco Chronicle* (April 10, 1881).

Charcoal portraits of John Brown and Mary Ann Day Brown by Sarah Brown. Collection of the Saratoga Historical Foundation, Saratoga, California.

Top: Mary Ann Day Brown with Annie on the left and Sarah on the right, circa 1851. Collection of the Saratoga Historical Foundation, Saratoga, California.
Below: Ellen Brown, circa 1864. Collection of the Saratoga Historical Foundation, Saratoga, California

CHAPTER III

1881 -1884
Saratoga, California

Twenty-one years passed since John Brown was hanged for his raid at Harpers Ferry. The news that his family would be moving to Saratoga spread quickly.

> Consternation and resentment echoed through the community at this startling news ... local Southerners "reacted bitterly ..." They had blamed John Brown with his consuming hatred of slavery as the instigator of the Civil War, and now his widow and her family were to become part of this peaceful community.[31]

The Brown party arrived late in the day on January 31, 1881. A group of southern sympathizers "who expressed the intention of hanging them"[32] awaited. They looked at three tired little girls, three women, and one tall slightly built man. Compassion reigned. Too late to ascend the mountain, the family "spent the night in the residence of John C. Hutchison, a person who was said to have shown sympathy for the

---

[31] Sarah Cunningham, *Saratoga's First One Hundred Years* (Fresno, California: Valley Publishers, 1967), 131.
[32] Garrod, 21.

Confederacy. The next morning he assisted them in the move up the mountain."[33]

Mary Brown and Ellen and her husband were pleased with Sarah's selection:

> … It is a mountain ranch, which my son-in-law wanted, and had a house already for occupancy, which I wanted … I like the mountain air, the grand view, and even the isolation. We can raise enough on this place to support us comfortably, and I think I could pass the rest of my days here pleasantly with my children and grandchildren."[34]

The property contained a small fruit orchard, and bushes of wild strawberries and blackberries were plentiful. Quail, rabbits, squirrels, and deer roamed the area. Mountain springs provided water, and the creeks teemed with trout. Wood was readily available to heat the small cabin. The smell of sage and bay leaf and laurel trees permeated the air. "In the spring wildflowers of every prismatic shade charmed the air everywhere, especially the rich, shimmering golden poppies, growing in wild abundance … Wild lilac, shooting star, lupine, wild violets, Indian paint-brush, mustard green and yellow were all … giving off a delicate fragrance."[35] There were other

---

[33] Nalty, 8.

[34] Mary Brown quoted in "John Brown's Widow, Visit to Her Mountain Home Near San Jose," *San Francisco Chronicle* (April 10, 1881).

[35] Cunningham, 223.

families in the mountain area. French, Swiss, and Italians had settled in the 1870s and planted the mountain in vineyards.[36]

The town itself bore an uncanny similarity to Saratoga, New York, close to where the Browns lived in the Adirondacks and where Sarah had attended school at Fort Edward Institute. Both were small mountain towns with beautiful rolling hills and healthy waters. In the 1850s, mineral springs were discovered close to the Bohlman Road property Mary would buy in 1880. Entrepreneurs bottled the water and sold it up and down the coast for "its medicinal qualities and invigorating flavor."[37] The content of the mineral water was identical to that of Congress Springs in Saratoga Springs, New York; hence, the name change of the town from McCartysville to Bank Mills to Saratoga.

In 1866, a resort hotel with cottages patterned after Congress Hall in New York was built and named the same. California artist Charles Nahl "vacationed here in the early seventies ... He was so enraptured with the miniature waterfalls tumbling down over the moss covered rocks by the soda springs that he vowed he would return soon and make a

---

36 Ibid., 212.
37 Ibid., 71.

painting of it!"[38] Could Sarah have heard of the beauty from Nahl?

The area was noted for its curative powers and the new hotel advertised "the baths are efficacious in cutaneous diseases and rheumatic affections. The waters, similar to Congress Springs, N.Y., are tonic, purgative, diuretic, alternative."[39] Mary Brown "once went on a medical retreat to a popular 'water cure.'[40] It could very well have been close to her home at Congress Springs, New York.

A home with fresh mountain air and curative springs close by could be the answer to James Fablinger's health. Mary may have felt the need for treatment herself. Cancer would claim her life in three years.

Saratoga was a bustling little lumber town with a population of 300.[41] Large wagons with seven-horse teams raced up and down dusty Lumber Street[42] with their large loads of wood. Heads would turn to watch as bells heralded their arrival. Stagecoaches traveled on Saratoga Avenue and along the small roads that branched off to Campbell, Moreland, Los Gatos, and the west side. Freight wagons, pedestrians, and

---

[38] Ibid.
[39] Ibid., 74.
[40] Libby, 15.
[41] San Jose City Directory, 1881-1882.
[42] Now Big Basin Way.

neighbors on horseback shared the road with sightseers visiting El Quito Olive Farm, the Sorosis Fruit Company, and Pacific Congress Springs. The Valley was awash in fruit trees and grape vines.

Although living on the mountain restricted their community activity, the Browns and Fablingers traveled up and down the mountain frequently. They were early members and lay leaders of the Congregational Church on Oak Street.[43]

Sarah helped Ellen with her nieces and resumed her artwork. She walked down the mountain giving music lessons and teaching painting and drawing. Charcoal was a medium she used in her art as it was plentiful.[44] James Fablinger added to the orchard, buying "grape cuttings and plum grafts" from Frank Farwell.[45] He obtained a teaching position at the Saratoga School on Oak Street at the foot of the mountain and "every day he walked down that mountain, taught school all day and then in the evening climbed back, frequently, I imagine, toting groceries in a sack over his shoulder."[46]

Sarah made friends easily. One of her closest and

---

[43] Garrod, 13.

[44] Ibid., "The making of charcoal was another industry that flourished in our Saratoga Mountains."

[45] Frank Farwell Diaries (December 21, 1881).

[46] Garrod, 13.

earliest friends was Lucy Higgins, wife of R. L. Higgins, the realtor who showed her the mountain property.

> One particular event occurred to make a friendship that I believe will be a life friendship … The day Miss Sarah Brown came to the office to inquire about the mountain home … my husband … brought her to us a stranger … and when Miss Brown came into our sitting room she found me trying to draw something that I wanted very badly to color. She came in laughing and we met her in the same spirit. She sat down by the fire and soon discovered what I was doing … volunteered to take the pencil and soon sketched … clear and distinct and I saw that our Sarah was an artist … She made herself so useful and so delightfully companionable we learned to love her and more than love … was a respect for a character so staunch and true in every principle of her life … that we have always been thankful that we had as fine an opportunity to know and admire her noble character.[47]

The Browns and the Fablingers hoped to distance themselves from the notoriety that came with being the family of John Brown; however, in April, shortly after they moved in, the San Jose newspaper ran a story suggesting that the widow of John Brown was living in poverty on top of the mountain and being taken care of by a daughter who was unprepared for the harsh farm work. The paper suggested that its readers help by contributing to pay off the mortgage.[48] On April 8th, two reporters ascended the mountain, one from the *San Jose Mercury* and another from the *San Francisco*

---

[47] Diary of Lucy Higgins. Higgins Family Collection.
[48] *San Jose Mercury* (March 30, 1881).

Chronicle, the latter riding a spirited mustang up "the steepest, most winding, roughest and uncompromising mountain trail … the reporter in all his news gather wanderings had every encountered.[49] They met Mrs. Brown, "a tall straight woman, apparently about 50 years of age, though fifteen years older than that. Her hair is only tinged with gray, but her face is furrowed by lines, sorrow-graven."[50] Mary told them, "I should willingly accept any such aid to clear our home from debt, if it came only from people who thought a debt of gratitude was due to the memory of John Brown."[51] Sarah entered the room and added:

> My mother … may have earned the right to expect some such aid, although she has never asked for it. She sent husband and two sons to that hopeless Virginia insurrection with her blessing, and prayed for them and the cause for which they gave their lives. She sympathized with every thought of my father and saw that the cause of freedom required a martyr, and when fate decreed her husband to be that martyr, she bowed her head submissively and prayed again for his cause.[52]

Sarah did not agree that she or other family members deserved any such money, "… but not to her family. I am able

---

[49] "John Brown's Widow, Visit to Her Mountain Home Near San Jose," *San Francisco Chronicle* (April 10, 1881).

[50] Ibid.

[51] Ibid.

[52] Ibid.

to take care of myself, and I would die before I would accept a penny which I had not earned from anyone."[53]

"The reporter was inclined to accept this literally when he afterwards learned that the lady walked into Saratoga, down that three-mile mountain trail and back, to give one music lesson."[54]

On May 18, 1881, less than four months after the family moved in, Mary Ann Brown acquired full title to the mountain property.[55] She immediately deeded one third to Ellen and one third to Sarah.[56]

The family remained on the mountain, but, in August 1882, Mary traveled back East to visit family in Ohio, Kansas, and New York where she would bury the remains of her son Watson who was killed twenty-three years earlier at Harpers Ferry under a flag of truce. Watson's body had been taken to a medical school for anatomical research.[57] Finally his remains came home, and he was buried beside his father at the farm in North Elba.

While she was gone, Sarah applied for and received a

---

[53] Ibid.
[54] Ibid.
[55] Santa Clara County Deeds, 59:578.
[56] Santa Clara County Deeds, 64:256, 258.
[57] Louis Ruchames, Ed. *A John Brown Reader* (New York:Abelard-Schuman, 1888), 407.

political appointment as an assistant weigher with the United States Mint in San Francisco. Sarah moved to the City. Mary returned from her trip back East.

> …her health was failing … She contemplated the sale of the property above Saratoga … Sarah was then living in San Francisco. James Fablinger was in poor health. The orchard required much attention and never quite came up to expectations. It was difficult to walk the winding road to the village, adding to the isolation of the place. This same problem hampered the visits by the doctor and those visits had been necessarily increasing. Mary Brown appeared to be a woman putting her affairs in order.[58]

In July of 1883, the property was sold.[59] Mary, Sarah, and Ellen then purchased "thirteen acres on Saratoga Avenue … Presently the site of Sacred Heart Church and School … and 8.3 acres fronting on McCall Road, now Fruitvale Avenue … Presently this is the site of the Saratoga Civic Center. These two parcels connected along Wildcat Creek."[60] Because there was no dwelling on the properties, they moved into a rented home at 13915 Saratoga Avenue.[61]

Mary moved to San Francisco to be with Sarah and close to medical attention. She died on February 29, 1884.

---

[58] Nalty, 24.
[59] Ibid., 24.
[60] Ibid., 26.
[61] Cunningham, 133.

> Mr. W. H. Cross called … saying Mrs. John Brown died yesterday in the City and her remains will come down this evening. Sarah, her daughter, will also come …[62]

> Jennie and I … found Sarah had come with her mother's remains. I took our light wagon and went down to Fablinger's and took up to the cemetery the rough box for the coffin and they selected a lot for the grave … Warm day, sultry. The fruit trees are beginning to come out.[63]

> No regular church service today at our church on account of the funeral of Mrs. John Brown which took place at 2 p.m. from the Congregational Church of which she was a member. A large number of people were present. Mr. Cross preached the sermon. Some signs of rain. Warm and cloudy. No wind.[64]

Mary Ann Day Brown was devoted to her husband and her children. She married John Brown at seventeen in 1833. He was thirty-three years old, a widower with five children under the age of twelve. "The elder children were always devoted to her."[65] She bore him thirteen more. Seven of those would die in childhood, and two were killed at Harpers Ferry. She was a strong, hardworking woman "of few words."[66] She endured her husband's frequent absences because "she was upheld by devotion to the cause … Without her, John Brown never could

---

[62] Diary of Frank Farwell (February 29, 1884).

[63] Ibid (March 1, 1884).

[64] Ibid (March 2, 1884).

[65] Katherine Mayo, "Interview with Sarah Brown, September 16-20, 1908," John Brown Papers, Columbia University Library.

[66] Ibid.

have done his work. She was as ready to sacrifice herself as he was in his own case …[67] As the Civil War waged on, she wrote, "Oh what a dreadful war that is … when I read of so much suffering I feel to cry out How Long Oh Lord how long shall this people continue in their sins and the innocent have to suffer with the guilty."[68]

She was a loving woman, devoted to her children, and her family grieved.

Sarah returned to San Francisco. "I like the work but was never very strong to endure close confinement … Sarah's work with the San Francisco Mint came to a halt with the election of Grover Cleveland in 1884 when she … was swept away in the purge of Republicans in government jobs by the first Democrat to be elected President since the Civil War …"[69]

---

[67] Ibid.

[68] John Brown's Family: A Living Legacy" *Civil War Times Magazine*, http://www.thehistorynet.com/ (February 25, 2005).

[69] Libby, Jean, 22.

CHAPTER IV

1884 -1916
Saratoga, California

Sarah moved in with the Fablingers to the rented house on Saratoga Avenue. It was a lively household. Ellen and James now had five children under the age of eight and three more would be born soon. James Fablinger continued to teach at the local school, and the whole family was involved in tending their orchard.

Sorosis Fruit Farm, Early 1890's, Sarah Brown on far right. Collection of the Saratoga Historical Foundation.

Sarah continued to paint and gave lessons to students in Saratoga, Los Gatos, Santa Clara, and elsewhere. Like many of the other women and children, she supplemented her income by working seasonally at the Sorosis Fruit Company, a short walk from her home. She is pictured packing fruit in a photograph taken in the early 1890's showing the inside of the Sorosis building.[70]

Lucy Higgins
The Higgins Family
Collection.

In 1886, Sarah and the Fablingers sold parts of the property they owned on Saratoga Avenue and lived on the property fronting Fruitvale.[71]

Lucy Higgins and
Sarah Brown
The Higgins Family
Collection.

Sarah may have used some of the proceeds to finance travel over the next few years for fun and to visit family. On June 11, 1888, she joined her good friend, Lucy Higgins, on a camping trip to Yosemite, a trip that for all its scenic beauty

---

[70] Cunningham, 151.
[71] Nalty, 37.

and camaraderie would appear to have some of the same pitfalls as camping today.[72]

> Camping the second night at a … charming place … Made our arrangements for the night on the bank of a made lake of water. The willow bent gracefully and shadowed itself in the water. A picture indeed with our white tent and blazing fire … As soon as we began to set out the food for our supper the flies like clouds began to hover over us. Then descending, took possession. Next the grunt of the festive hog was heard. Between these two pests and a loose soil that rose light and airy at the slightest breeze had become a strong wind. With the tent tied down closely, everything covered from the invading flies and pigs we retired into our canvas home.[73]

In 1890 Sarah traveled down to Pasadena to visit her sister Ruth, and, in 1893, she traveled to the East Coast to visit family and friends, spending some time in Concord, Massachusetts, revisiting places and friends from her childhood.

> In 1893 after thirty-one years, I returned to Concord but besides my teacher, Mr. Sanborn, I found only a few of those I had once known. Mr. Robertson James, a brother of the novelist and a daughter of Judge Hoar were the only ones of the school who were there … Mr. Sanborn gave me a ride about the town which is much the same with the same old elm trees. The homes of the Emersons, Alcotts, Hawthornes, Thoreaus were still there …[74]

---

[72] Diary of Lucy Higgins (June 11, 1888).

[73] Ibid.

[74] Sarah Brown, "A Reminiscence," Collection of the Saratoga Historical Foundation.

James Fablinger no longer taught school and worked full time in his orchard. Unfortunately, the fruit boom of the 1880's gave way to a depression in the 1890's. He found additional work as secretary at the Fairview Evaporating and Canning Company,[75] but the family continued to have difficulties and sold the property fronting Fruitvale Avenue in 1895.[76] That year, the Fablingers started a new life in Ben Lomond. Settling there in the same year was Sarah's brother, Jason Brown.[77]

Sarah remained in possession of a small piece of land fronting Saratoga Avenue and widening back toward the creek. A house had been built on the adjacent property that Sarah and the Fablingers had sold in 1886 and Sarah was able to rent it.[78] She had always helped with the orchard, but now she had its full responsibility.

> Saratoga had become a quiet little farming center by the turn of the century … Everyone, especially the young people, derived great enjoyment from even simple pleasures … there was much friendly visiting and as many social functions as the busy farmers and villagers had time to attend.[79]

---

[75] Nalty, 37.
[76] Ibid.
[77] Ibid., 93.
[78] Ibid., 36.
[79] Cunningham, 240.

In 1900 the Fablingers returned and lived with Sarah for a short while on Saratoga Avenue, but they moved to Campbell in 1902. When the house Sarah rented was sold, James Fablinger returned in 1905 to build her a small dwelling.

She now had her own home on her property beside the little creek. It was quiet and peaceful amid the fruit trees, and Sarah painted "Basket of Apples," a small pastel still life that she gave to her good friend and fellow Congregational Church parishioner, Jessie Pendleton.[80] Amanda Cunningham was given a pastel landscape showing Mt. Diablo.[81] The Saratoga Historical Foundation owns two charcoal portraits of Sarah's mother and father, a mission study, and a still-life painting of a branch of peaches. Another painting hangs on the wall of the Kelly-Griggs House Museum in Red Bluff.

In the following years, Sarah, "in spite of her many varied personal activities … always found time to help in church, club, and other community affairs."[82] She was a member of the Saratoga Foothill Club and participated in 1912 in "The Club's most spectacular project … the Blossom Festival … a pageant depicting high points in California's

---

[80] Collection of the Saratoga Historical Foundation.

[81] Ibid.

[82] *After Harper's Ferry* (Saratoga, California: Saratoga Historical Foundation, 1964), 7.

colorful history … the whole community … joined the project … Included were Indians, Mission Padres, caballeros, senoritas, miners and pack train, and an overland emigrant train with an ox-drawn covered wagon in which Study Club member Miss Sarah Brown … rode …"[83]

It was the ox-drawn covered wagon that stole the show. In it rode Sarah Brown wearing a replica of the calico dress and old-fashioned sun bonnet she had worn nearly fifty years before when she had traveled in a similar covered wagon across the plains of California."[84]

Sarah Brown, Saratoga Blossom Festival, 1912. Collection of the Saratoga Historical Foundation, Saratoga, California.

---

[83] The Saratoga Foothill Club, A History.
[84] Cunningham, 285.

She also was a member of the Women's Relief Corps of Los Gatos and presented a picture of her mother to them and one of her father to the E.O.C. Ord Post. An item in the *San Jose Mercury* on August 21, 1903 described her visit to San Francisco.

Sarah Brown, Saratoga Blossom Festival, 1912. Collection of the Saratoga Historical Foundation, Saratoga, California.

John Brown's daughter, Miss Sarah Brown, whose father was the famous abolitionist ... John Brown, the hero of history and song, was the center of an admiring coterie yesterday afternoon at the Press Committee's Grand Army of the Republic headquarters at the "Grand Hotel"... Miss Brown, accompanied by her niece, Miss Vera Brown Fablinger, is a woman of strong and pleasing personality, with every indication that she inherited her father's firm and kindly nature. This is her first visit to an encampment and she has been a member of the Women's Relief Corps ... Miss Brown moved to Saratoga, California where she follows the occupation of a ranch woman.[85]

---

[85] *San Jose Mercury* (August 21, 1903).

Sarah was a well-educated woman. Katherine Mayo described her as … "a lady of the old New England type, reserved and quiet-mannered, while full of kindliness and force. She is fond of books and reading, and of the traditions of the old days, when for a time, she lived in Concord and knew it at its best."[86] In 1902, she reminisced about her earlier life in Massachusetts when she attended Franklin Sanborn's school. "Living in Concord were many interesting people … there were the descendants of the Revolutionary heroes; and the buildings, streets and bridges have their stories…"[87]

Sarah had always been active in the Congregational Church and their Missionary Society. In 1891, she was chosen as one of eight delegates to attend the Annual Convention held in San Francisco on October 6th.[88] She participated in their study groups and gave a talk to its members on the earliest missions in China.[89] Like her father, she was a strong believer in God, and she supported their work in China, especially the Christian Kindergarten School.

---

[86] Katherine Mayo, "Interview with Sarah Brown, September 16 – 20, 1908," John Brown Papers, Columbia University Library.
[87] Sarah Brown, "A Reminiscence," Collection of the Saratoga Historical Foundation.
[88] Minutes of the Women's Home Missionary Society of the Congregational Church (September 16, 1891).
[89] Ibid (April 25, 1905).

When it became known that the building the school rented was sold:

> Miss Brown objected to [the school] going to another part of the city because then the same children could not come to … [the teacher] and she … asked for $6000 to erect a suitable building for school and rooms in rear she [teacher] could live.[90]

Unfortunately, only $3,000 was allotted for this project.

> When the matter was presented to the meeting of the South Branch, Miss Porter who had so strongly urged us to enter open doors, seemed to open wide this one and pledged the $3000 for the building as a memorial to her mother … Miss Brown has the full amount she asked for. A lesson in faith.[91]

In 1906, Sarah would find the meaning and mission that drove the remainder of her life.

> The idea was suggested to me several summers ago by a Japanese boy who I had working for me, and who became a convert. He urged hard that I should teach 'salvation' to some of his countrymen and promised that he would build with his own hands a meeting place if I would consent to instruct them. I had really no purpose in life and something said to me here was my opportunity to accomplish good. I agreed, and though I knew little or nothing of the Japanese language I found it not so very difficult to learn and by degrees I obtained a sufficient smattering to enable me to teach my pupils how to read and write in English and how to understand the bible and sing such hymns as I thought would best please them. My class proved very popular, and from one student it grew to seventeen and we met sometimes at the Congregational Church, sometimes at my home, and sometimes when the

---

90 Ibid (October 19, 1905).
91 Ibid.

class was very large we gathered together in the Japanese laundry and I taught the boys there with big bundles of washing for desks.[92]

In 1907 she was accredited by the American Missionary Society in San Francisco and remained very active supporting the Japanese Mission in San Francisco.

> The question of raising money for the support of the Japanese Mission in San Francisco from which societies of our church had received an appeal through Miss Brown … pledge herself to pay 5 cents or more a month to help support this mission.[93]

The work continued:

The matter of money to go to Miss Brown's Japanese friends in San Francisco was spoken of. The ladies were instructed to hand their contributions …[94]

Sarah would take no money for her work, but "many signs" about the house and garden attest the gratitude of her pupils…[95]

> Tucked away in a fold of the Saratoga foothills … a quaint little bungalow shelters nightly a class of … Japanese who are learning how to read and write and sing the battle hymn of the Republic to the accompaniment of a wheezy old reed organ, played enthusiastically by no less a personage than Sarah Brown, daughter of John

---

[92] Gerald P. Beaumont, "A Daughter of John Brown" *Sunset Magazine* (November 11, 1909).
[93] Minutes (February 21, 1911).
[94] Minutes (November 19, 1911).
[95] "Sturdy Children of John Brown," *The New York Evening Post* (November 6, 1909).

> Brown of Harper's Ferry … For Sarah Brown … has become a missionary and converted her picturesque little hermitage to a school … She told me … "I am working under the auspices of the American Missionary Association, and I plan to spend the remaining years of my life here, doing what I can for the people I have learned to love."[96]

"Sarah's work with the Japanese laborers reflected her spirituality and her humanity, but in this time and place it also reflected her courage … Asian immigrants were the targets of prejudice in California. The issue came to a clear focus when the San Francisco public school system ordered segregation of all 'Oriental' pupils."[97] Sarah strongly resembled her father. "I respect and honor my father's memory for his lesson to the world of self-sacrifice."[98] She also resembled him physically. While living in Concord, Massachusetts, after her father's death, "She frequently saw the frail Henry David Thoreau at the Post Office and perhaps unwittingly contributed to these words of his: 'Of all the men who were said to be my contemporaries, it seems to me that John Brown is the only one who has not died. I meet him at every turn. He is more alive than he ever was."[99]

---

[96] Beaumont.
[97] Nalty, 46-47.
[98] Sarah Brown, *Springfield Republican* (May 15, 1905).
[99] Libby, 22.

In a 1909 interview with Sarah Brown, Katherine Mayo wrote:

> Her delicate but strongly marked, aquiline features and the classic lines of her head seem but a feminine version of that strong prototype, and as she talks, expressions flit across her face that bring back with almost startling force expressions of John Brown's own …[100]

Sarah tried to remain for as long as she could in her home beside the creek next to her fruit orchard. She participated in as many community activities as she could and, with the help of her devoted Japanese students, she tended the orchard. In 1915, she could not continue. Breast cancer was slowly ebbing her life away. She moved in with her sister, Ellen, in Campbell so they could nurse her. Ellen was also suffering from the same disease.

Sarah Brown died on June 30, 1916. Within a month, Ellen would also be dead. Both sisters are buried beside their mother in Madronia Cemetery.

Grave of
Sarah Brown and
Ellen Brown Fablinger.
Photographer: Chiao

---

[100] "Sturdy Children of John Brown," *The New York Evening Post* (November 6, 1909).

Sarah Brown

Sarah Brown, Collection of the Saratoga Historical Foundation, Saratoga, California.

CHAPTER V

2022
Saratoga, California

> "Follow this road, and when you come to the end of it about three miles from here, and at the very ridge of the mountains, you will find the widow Brown's place"… The air was soft and warm; the insects hummed dreamily; lizards sunning themselves on the rocks, darted beneath shelter at the sound of hoofs; the odor of the wildflowers made the gentle breeze heavy with their weight of sweetness … Yet the great ascent was hundred times repaid by the beauty … Three miles on a road stood on end and zigzagged into every canyon and round every jutting spur lead at last at last above the trees to the highest ridge, surmounting which stood the last cottage of the martyred patriot's widow.[101]

The floor of the Santa Clara Valley was covered with fruit trees in the 1880's. In springtime, Sarah and her family could look down from the mountain and see the entire valley covered in blossoms, like a pastel painting.

Today the road that leads up the mountain is still a challenging drive, narrow and windy with hairpin turns. Houses are tucked behind long driveways that disappear into

---

[101] "John Brown's Widow, Visit To Her Mountain Home Near San Jose," *San Francisco Chronicle* (April 10, 1881).

the trees. There are glimpses of a valley now covered with buildings. In later years, an entrepreneur built a two-story cabin on the site of Sarah's home. It was advertised and known locally as the "John Brown Lodge," even though John Brown and his family never lived in it. Locals remember picnics on the "John Brown Mountain." For a while, the property was a boy scout camp.

In 1883, Sarah and her family moved down from the mountain. They lived and tended their orchards on Saratoga Avenue and Fruitvale.

If you stand in the middle of Saratoga's beautiful Heritage Orchard and look up, you can see the top of "John Brown Mountain." Sarah Brown could do that over one hundred years ago.

ACKNOWLEDGEMENTS

Special thank you to April Halberstadt, former Executive Director of the Saratoga Museum, for opening up the doors, giving suggestions, and always being available.

Special thank you to Mrs. Damon G. Nalty.

Jean Libby for advice and a walk through the cemetery and the Saratoga Avenue and Fruitvale areas where Sarah and Ellen lived.

Lori Deal and the Higgins Family for sharing their treasures.

David Satterthwaite for sharing "Basket of Apples."

All the wonderful historians, research assistants, librarians, and history lovers who want the past to remain alive.

BIBLIOGRAPHY

ARTICLES

Beaumont, Gerald P., "A Daughter of John Brown," *Sunset Magazine,* November 11, 1911.

Cotter, Edwin N., Jr., "John Brown in the Adirondacks," *Adirondack Life Magazine,* Summer 1972.

"Her Only Time---Widow Brown Visited in 1883," *Osawatomie Graphic*, July 11, 1996.

"John Brown's Family: A Living Legacy," *Civil War Times Magazine*, February 25, 2005, http://www.thehistorynet.com/.

"John Brown's Widow: Visit to Her Mountain Home Near San Jose," *San Francisco Chronicle,* April 10, 1881.

"John Brown's Wife Called Saratoga Home," *Los Gatos/Saratoga Observer*, September 28, 1976.

Libby, Jean, "John Brown's Family and Their California Refuge," *The Californians*, vol. 7, no. 1, 1989.

Libby, Jean, "Commemorating Brown and Turner in Northern California," *New Abolitionist, Inc.*, Dorchester, MA 02122 199, newabolition@racetraitor.

Moody, Linda A., Mills College, "Religio-Political Insights of 19th Century Women Hymnists and Lyric Poets," *Janus Head*, March 12, 2005, http://www.janushead.org/JHSumm99/moody.cfin/.

"Oat Creek School," *Tehama County Memories 1987,* Red Bluff: Tehama County Genealogical and Historical Society, 1987.

"The Passing of Sarah Brown, Daughter of John Brown of Harper's Ferry, A Pioneer of Saratoga," *Saratoga Record,* July 7, 1916.

Peck, Willys, "Brown an Early Advocate for Japanese Community," *Saratoga News,* April 23, 2003.

Peck, Willys, "Brown Family---Minus John---In Madronia Cemetery," *Saratoga News*, March 26, 2003.

Peck, Willys, "Brown's Iron Will Inherited by His Daughter Sarah," *Saratoga News,* April 9, 2003.

"Sturdy Children of John Brown," *The New York Evening Post,* November 6, 1909.

"The Late Miss Sarah Brown," *San Jose Mercury Herald,* July 2, 1916.

"Threats, Then Friends, For John Brown's People," *Los Gatos Daily Times*, March 26, 1953.

Tiedeman, John E, "Widow of John Brown Found Sanctuary Atop Saratoga Hill," *San Francisco Examiner,* January 9, 1927.

"Widow of Famed Abolitionist Brown: Her Final Resting Place in Saratoga," *San Jose Mercury News,* February 9, 1965.

"Unmarked Frame House in Red Bluff Was Home of John Brown's Widow," *Sacramento Bee*, October 31, 1975.

Walther, Lou, "The Brown House," *Tehama County Memories 1990*, Red Bluff: Tehama County Genealogical and Historical Society, 1990.

Williams, Rev. Edward Sidney, "John Brown's Spirit in the Santa Clara Foothills," *Overland Monthly,* vol. 54, September 1909.

BOOKS

Clark, Tom Foran. *The Significance of Being Frank*. February 22, 2005. http://www.ameribilia.com/sanborn/chapter8.html/.

BOOKS Continued

Cunningham, Sarah. *Saratoga's First Hundred Years*. California: Valley Publishers, 1967.

Garrod, R. V. *Saratoga Story*. Privately published, 1961.

Muir, John, Ed. *Picturesque California: The Rocky Mountains and the Pacific Slope*. New York: The J Dewing Co., 1888.

Nalty, Damon G. *The Browns of Madonia*. Saratoga: Saratoga Historical Foundation, 1996.

Renehan, Edward J., Jr. *The Secret Six*. New York: Crown Publishers, Inc., 1995.

Ruchames, Louis., Ed. *A John Brown Reader*. New York: Abelard-Schuman, 1988.

Saratoga Historical Foundation. *After Harper's Ferry*. Saratoga: Saratoga Historical Foundation, 1964.

OTHER

Boyd B. Stuttler Letter to Florence Cunningham, August 1962, Collection of the Saratoga Historical Foundation.

Charlotte Cunningham Letter to Sarah Cunningham, August 1963, Collection of the Saratoga Historical Foundation.

Clarence S. Gee Letter to Florence Cunningham, August 1962, Collection of the Saratoga Historical Foundation.

Diaries of Frank Farwell, Collection of the Saratoga Historical Foundation.

Diary of Lucy Higgins, Higgins Family Collection.

John Brown Farm Pamphlet, State Historic Site, Lake Placid, New York, 30 September 1983.

Minutes of the Women's Missionary Society of the Congregational Church, Collection of the Saratoga Federated Church.

Red Bluff Independent, 24 April, 1 May, 8 May 1867, Advertisements.

San Jose City Directory, 1881 – 1882.

Santa Clara County Deeds.

Sarah Brown, "A Reminiscence," Collection of the Saratoga Historical Foundation.

Sarah Brown, Interview by Katherine Mayo, 16-20 September 1908, John Brown Papers: Sarah Brown File, Special Collections, The Columbia University Libraries.

Sarah Cunningham letter to Charlotte Cunningham, August 31, 1963, Collection of the Saratoga Historical Foundation. Saratoga Foothill Club, A History

About the Author

Mary Miller Chiao has won awards for historical research from the California Pioneers of Santa Clara County. *Adirondack Life Magazine* published her memoir of summers in the Adirondack Mountains in the 1950s, and an album of material from that time frame has been on display at the Kinnear Museum in Lake Luzerne, New York.

She is the author of *Death on the Funeral Yacht, A 1950s San Francisco Mystery.* Her fiction appears in *The California Writers Club Literary Review, Good Old Days, WritersTalk,* and *Carry the Light.* She has won literary competitions at the San Mateo County Fair and the National League of American Pen Women, Nob Hill, San Francisco branch.

She is a member of the National League of American Pen Women, the California Writers Club, both the Peninsula and South Bay Branches, and she is a contributing editor to *WritersTalk.*

She resides in Northern California.

MaryMillerChiao@gmail.com
http://www.MaryMillerChiao.com